Incredibly Easy
Recipes

Publications International, Ltd.

Favorite Brand Name Recipes at www.fbnr.com

Special thanks to the Campbell's Kitchen, Lucinda Ayers, Vice President, and Catherine Marschean-Spivak, Group Manager.

Photography on pages 5, 7, 15, 19, 21, 23, 25, 27, 39, 41, 43, 49, 69, 71, 73, 75, 77, 79, 81, 83, 85, 87, 89, 99, 101, 103, 105, 107, 127, and 129 by Stephen Hamilton Photographics, Inc., Chicago.

Pictured on front cover: Creamy Vegetable Penne (*page 26*).

Pictured on back cover (clockwise from top): Swiss-Style Veal and Mushrooms (*page 102*), Sun-Dried Tomato Risotto (*page 38*), and Herb Roasted Chicken & Vegetables (*page 112*).

ISBN 13: 978-1-4127-2915-4
ISBN 10: 1-4127-2915-7

Manufactured in China.

8 7 6 5 4 3 2 1

Microwave Cooking: Microwave ovens vary in wattage. Use the cooking times as guidelines and check for doneness before adding more time.

Preparation/Cooking Times: Preparation times are based on the approximate amount of time required to assemble the recipe before cooking, baking, chilling or serving. These times include preparation steps such as measuring, chopping and mixing. The fact that some preparations and cooking can be done simultaneously is taken into account. Preparation of optional ingredients and serving suggestions is not included.

Contents

Homemade in Minutes

Bring out the homemade taste in a matter of minutes.

Turkey Piccata

MAKES: 4 SERVINGS

PREP: 5 MINUTES

COOK: 20 MINUTES

1 lemon

1 tablespoon olive oil

4 turkey breast cutlets **or** slices

1 medium onion, chopped (about ½ cup)

1 can (10¾ ounces) Campbell's® Condensed Cream of Chicken Soup (Regular **or** 98% Fat Free)

½ cup milk

2 tablespoons cooked crumbled bacon

Hot cooked rice

CAMPBELL'S KITCHEN

tip

For the amount of bacon needed, use 1 slice bacon, cooked and crumbled, or bacon bits.

1. Cut 4 thin slices of lemon. Squeeze **2 teaspoons** juice from the remaining lemon. Set aside

2. Heat the oil in a 12-inch skillet over medium-high heat. Add the turkey in 2 batches and cook for 3 minutes or until the turkey is lightly browned on both sides. Remove the turkey.

3. Add the onion and cook until tender.

4. Stir the soup, milk and reserved lemon juice into the skillet. Heat to a boil. Return the turkey to the skillet and reduce the heat to low. Top the turkey with the lemon slices. Cover and cook for 5 minutes or until the turkey is cooked through. Sprinkle with the bacon. Serve with rice.

Presto Parmesan

MAKES: 6 SERVINGS

PREP: 5 MINUTES

BAKE: 25 MINUTES

2¾ cups Prego® Traditional Italian Sauce

6 frozen cooked breaded chicken breast fillets

2 tablespoons grated Parmesan cheese

1 cup shredded mozzarella cheese (4 ounces)

1. Pour **1 cup** of the sauce in a 13×9-inch (3-quart) shallow baking dish. Top with the chicken, remaining sauce and cheeses. **Cover**.

2. Bake at 400°F. for 20 minutes. Uncover and bake 5 minutes more or until the cheese is lightly browned.

Pesto Pizza Parmesan: Top the chicken with ½ cup *chopped pepperoni* before baking.

Balsamic Glazed Salmon

MAKES: 8 SERVINGS

PREP: 5 MINUTES

BAKE: 15 MINUTES

COOK: 5 MINUTES

CAMPBELL'S KITCHEN

When grating citrus fruits, you'll want to avoid rubbing too deeply into the peel. There's a white layer between the outer peel and the flesh, called the pith, which can be bitter.

8   fresh salmon fillets, ¾-inch thick (about 1½ pounds)
     Freshly ground black pepper
3   tablespoons olive oil
4½   teaspoons cornstarch
1¾   cups Swanson® Chicken Broth (Regular, Natural Goodness™ **or** Certified Organic)
3   tablespoons balsamic vinegar
1   tablespoon brown sugar
1   tablespoon orange juice
1   teaspoon grated orange peel
     Orange slices for garnish (optional)

1. Place the salmon in an 11×8-inch (2-quart) shallow baking dish. Sprinkle with black pepper and drizzle with the oil. Bake at 350°F. for 15 minutes or until the fish flakes easily when tested with a fork.

2. Stir the cornstarch, broth, vinegar, brown sugar, orange juice and orange peel in a 2-quart saucepan over high heat to a boil. Cook and stir until the mixture boils and thickens.

3. Place the salmon on a serving platter and serve with the sauce. Garnish with the orange slices, if desired.

Beef Stroganoff

MAKES: 4 SERVINGS

PREP: 10 MINUTES

COOK: 20 MINUTES

1 pound boneless beef sirloin **or** top round steak, ¾-inch thick, cut into 2-inch pieces

Cracked black pepper

1 tablespoon vegetable oil

1 medium onion, finely chopped (about ½ cup)

1 can (10¾ ounces) Campbell's® Condensed Cream of Mushroom Soup (Regular **or** 98% Fat Free)

½ cup water

¼ cup dry sherry (optional)

1 tablespoon tomato paste

¼ cup plain yogurt

Hot cooked medium egg noodles

Chopped fresh parsley

1. Sprinkle the beef with the black pepper.

2. Heat the oil in a 10-inch skillet over medium-high heat. Add the beef and cook until it's well browned on all sides, stirring often. Remove the beef with a slotted spoon and set it aside.

3. Reduce the heat to medium. Add the onion and cook until tender.

4. Stir the soup, water, sherry, if desired, and tomato paste into the skillet. Heat to a boil. Return the beef to the skillet and heat through. Remove from the heat. Stir in the yogurt. Serve over the noodles and sprinkle with the parsley.

Chicken & Broccoli Alfredo

MAKES: 4 SERVINGS

PREP: 10 MINUTES

COOK: 15 MINUTES

½ of a 16-ounce package linguine

1 cup fresh **or** frozen broccoli flowerets

2 tablespoons butter

1 pound skinless, boneless chicken breasts, cut into cubes

1 can (10¾ ounces) Campbell's® Condensed Cream of Mushroom Soup (Regular **or** 98% Fat Free)

½ cup milk

½ cup grated Parmesan cheese

¼ teaspoon ground black pepper

EASY SUBSTITUTION

Use spaghetti for the linguine.

1. Prepare the linguine according to the package directions in a 3-quart saucepan. Add the broccoli during the last 4 minutes of the cooking time. Drain the linguine and broccoli well in a colander.

2. Heat the butter in a 10-inch skillet over medium-high heat. Add the chicken and cook until it's well browned, stirring often.

3. Stir the soup, milk, cheese, black pepper and linguine mixture into the skillet. Cook until the mixture is hot and bubbling, stirring occasionally. Serve with additional Parmesan cheese, if desired.

Pan-Seared Chicken with Red Grapes

MAKES: 4 SERVINGS

PREP: 10 MINUTES

COOK: 20 MINUTES

1 tablespoon olive oil

4 skinless, boneless chicken breasts

1 clove garlic, minced

1 cup Swanson® Chicken Broth (Regular, Natural Goodness™ **or** Certified Organic)

½ teaspoon Italian seasoning, crushed

1 tablespoon balsamic vinegar

2 cups seedless red grapes

Hot cooked bow tie-shaped pasta (farfalle)

CAMPBELL'S KITCHEN

At times of the year when red grapes are larger, you may cut the grapes in half for more bite-sized pieces.

1. Heat the oil in a 10-inch skillet over medium-high heat. Add the chicken and cook for 10 minutes or until it's well browned on both sides. Add the garlic and cook for 30 seconds. Remove the chicken.

2. Increase the heat to high. Stir the broth and Italian seasoning into the skillet. Add the vinegar and cook for 3 minutes.

3. Return the chicken to the skillet. Reduce the heat to low. Cook for 5 minutes or until the chicken is cooked through. Add the grapes. Serve with pasta.

Mozzarella Meatball Sandwiches

MAKES: 4 SANDWICHES

PREP: 5 MINUTES

BAKE: 10 MINUTES

COOK: 20 MINUTES

1 loaf (11.75 ounces) Pepperidge Farm® Frozen Mozzarella & Garlic Cheese Bread

½ cup Prego® Traditional **or** Organic Tomato & Basil Italian Sauce

12 (½ ounce **each**) **or** 6 (1 ounce **each**) frozen meatballs

1. Heat the oven to 400°F.

2. Remove the bread from the bag. Place the frozen bread halves, cut-side up, on an ungreased baking sheet. (If the bread halves are frozen together, carefully insert a fork between halves to separate.) Place baking sheet on the middle oven rack.

3. Bake for 10 minutes or until it's hot.

4. Heat the sauce and meatballs in a 2-quart saucepan over low heat. Cook and stir for 20 minutes or until the meatballs are heated through.

5. Place the meatballs onto the bottom bread half. Top with the remaining bread half. Cut into quarters.

Inside Out Pizza Casserole

MAKES: 6 SERVINGS

PREP: 20 MINUTES

BAKE: 30 MINUTES

STAND: 10 MINUTES

½ of a 15-ounce package refrigerated pie crusts (1 crust)

1 tablespoon vegetable oil

1 pound bulk pork sausage

1 package (8 ounces) sliced mushrooms

1 large sweet onion, chopped (about 1 cup)

1½ cups Prego® Traditional Italian Sauce

4 ounces sliced pepperoni, coarsely chopped

1 package (8 ounces) shredded mozzarella cheese (2 cups)

½ cup grated Parmesan cheese

CAMPBELL'S KITCHEN

Use lightly floured star or other cookie cutter to make decorative shapes in pie crust before placing over sausage mixture.

1. Heat the oven to 400°F. Let the pie crust stand at room temperature for 15 minutes or until it's easy to handle.

2. Heat the oil in a 10-inch skillet over medium-high heat. Add the sausage and cook until it's well browned, stirring frequently to break up the meat.

3. Add the mushrooms and onion and cook until tender. Add the sauce and pepperoni. Cook for about 3 minutes or until the mixture is hot and bubbling. Remove from the heat and cool slightly. Stir in the mozzarella and Parmesan cheeses. Spoon the mixture into a 2-quart casserole or a deep-dish 9-inch pie plate.

4. Place the crust over the sausage mixture and flute the edges. Cut several slits in the top of the crust.

5. Bake for 30 minutes or until golden brown. Let the pie stand for 10 minutes before serving.

Chipotle Pork Tortilla Cups

MAKES: 10 TORTILLA CUPS

PREP: 10 MINUTES

BAKE: 5 MINUTES

COOK: 5 MINUTES

Vegetable cooking spray

10 (6-inch) whole wheat **or** flour tortillas

1 container (18 ounces) refrigerated cooked barbecue sauce with shredded pork (about 2 cups)

1 cup Pace® Chipotle **or** plain Chunky Salsa

Shredded Cheddar cheese (optional)

Guacamole (optional)

Sour cream (optional)

Sliced ripe olives (optional)

TIME-SAVING

tip

To save prep time, prepare the tortillas through step 3 ahead of time.

1. Heat the oven to 350°F. Spray 2 (3-inch) muffin-pan cups with cooking spray.

2. Wrap the tortillas between sheets of damp paper towels. Microwave on HIGH for 30 seconds until warm and softened. Fold **1** tortilla into thirds to form a cone shape. Open the center of cone and press the tortilla into a 3-inch muffin-pan cup. Repeat with remaining tortillas, rewarming as necessary.

3. Bake for 5 minutes or until golden. Remove from pan and set aside.

4. While tortillas are browning, heat the pork and salsa in a 2-quart saucepan over medium heat until the mixture is hot, stirring often.

5. Spoon about ¼ **cup** of the mixture into each cone-shaped tortilla. Top with cheese, guacamole, sour cream or olives, if desired.

Creamy Pork Marsala with Fettuccine

MAKES: 4 SERVINGS

PREP: 5 MINUTES

COOK: 25 MINUTES

1 tablespoon olive oil

4 boneless pork chops, ¾-inch thick

1 cup sliced mushrooms

1 clove garlic, minced

1 can (10¾ ounces) Campbell's® Condensed Cream of Mushroom Soup (Regular **or** 98% Fat Free)

½ cup milk

2 tablespoons dry Marsala wine

½ of a 16-ounce package spinach fettuccine pasta, cooked and drained

1. Heat the oil in a 10-inch skillet over medium-high heat. Add the pork chops and cook until they're well browned on both sides.

2. Add the mushrooms and garlic to the skillet and cook until tender.

3. Stir the soup, milk and wine into the skillet. Heat to a boil. Reduce the heat to low. Cover and cook for 5 minutes or until the chops are cooked through. Serve with the pasta.

Brunch Bruschetta

MAKES: 4 SERVINGS

PREP: 20 MINUTES

COOL: 5 MINUTES

**EASY
SUBSTITUTION**

**Peaches & Cream
Bruschetta:**
*Substitute chopped
fresh peaches for the
strawberries.*

4 Pepperidge Farm® Frozen Hearth Fired Artisan
    Hearty Wheat Rolls

2 tablespoons honey

8 fresh strawberries, stemmed and chopped
    (about 1 cup)

1 cup fresh blueberries

2 tablespoons orange juice

1 tablespoon chopped fresh mint

⅓ cup vanilla yogurt

1. Prepare the rolls according to the package directions.
Remove from the baking sheet and cool for 5 minutes on
a wire rack. Cut in half. Return to the oven and bake for
5 minutes or until lightly toasted. Drizzle **1 tablespoon** of
the honey over the roll halves.

2. Put the strawberries, blueberries, **1 tablespoon** of the
orange juice and mint in a small bowl. Toss to coat. Divide
the berry mixture among the rolls.

3. Stir the yogurt with the remaining honey and remaining
orange juice in a small bowl. Spoon the yogurt mixture
over the berries. Serve immediately.

Creamy Vegetable Penne

MAKES: 4 SERVINGS

PREP: 10 MINUTES

COOK: 20 MINUTES

2 tablespoons olive oil

1 bag (16 ounces) frozen vegetable combination (broccoli, cauliflower, carrots), thawed

3 cloves garlic, minced

1 can (10¾ ounces) Campbell's® Condensed Cream of Mushroom Soup (Regular **or** 98% Fat Free)

1 teaspoon dried basil leaves, crushed

1 can (about 15 ounces) diced tomatoes, undrained

2½ cups medium tube-shaped pasta (penne), cooked and drained

Grated Parmesan cheese

1. Heat the oil in a 12-inch skillet over medium-high heat. Add the vegetables and garlic and cook for 2 minutes.

2. Stir the soup, basil and tomatoes into the skillet. Heat to a boil. Reduce the heat to low. Cover and cook for 10 minutes or until the vegetables are tender.

3. Spoon the pasta into a large serving bowl. Top with the vegetable mixture. Toss to coat. Sprinkle with Parmesan cheese.

Beef Taco Bake

MAKES: 4 SERVINGS

PREP: 10 MINUTES

BAKE: 30 MINUTES

1 pound ground beef

1 can (10¾ ounces) Campbell's® Condensed Tomato Soup

1 cup chunky salsa **or** picante sauce

½ cup milk

6 (8-inch) flour tortillas, cut into 1-inch pieces **or** 8 (6-inch) corn tortillas, cut into 1-inch pieces

1 cup shredded Cheddar cheese (4 ounces)

1. Cook the beef in a 10-inch skillet over medium-high heat until the beef is well browned, stirring frequently to break up meat. Pour off any fat.

2. Stir the soup, salsa, milk, tortillas and **half** the cheese into the skillet. Spoon into an 11×8-inch (2-quart) shallow baking dish. **Cover**.

3. Bake at 400°F. for 30 minutes or until hot. Sprinkle with the remaining cheese.

Longevity Noodle Soup

MAKES: 8 SERVINGS

PREP: 10 MINUTES

COOK: 15 MINUTES

4   teaspoons cornstarch

2   tablespoons water

1   tablespoon sesame oil

8   cups Swanson® Chicken Broth (Regular, Natural Goodness™ **or** Certified Organic)

3   tablespoons soy sauce

2   eggs, beaten

1   package (16 ounces) thin spaghetti, cooked and drained

¼   pound sliced cooked ham, cut into 2-inch-long strips (about 1 cup)

4   medium green onions, chopped (about ½ cup)

1. Stir the cornstarch, water and sesame oil in a small cup. Set the mixture aside.

2. Heat the broth and soy sauce in a 3-quart saucepan over medium-high heat to a boil. Stir the cornstarch mixture and stir it into the saucepan. Cook and stir until mixture is slightly thickened.

3. Reduce the heat to low. Add the eggs in a slow steady stream, stirring while adding. Remove the saucepan from the heat. Divide the spaghetti, ham and green onions among **8** serving bowls. Ladle **about 1 cup** of the broth mixture into each bowl. Serve immediately.

Mediterranean Couscous

MAKES: 4 SERVINGS

PREP: 5 MINUTES

COOK: 10 MINUTES

STAND: 5 MINUTES

1 cup Swanson® Vegetable **or** Chicken Broth

½ teaspoon grated lemon peel

½ teaspoon Italian seasoning, crushed

8 to 10 asparagus spears (about ½ pound), cut into 1-inch pieces (about 1½ cups)

1 can (14.5 ounces) diced tomatoes, drained

¾ cup **uncooked** plain instant couscous

1. Heat the broth, lemon peel, Italian seasoning, asparagus and tomatoes in a 2-quart saucepan over medium-high heat to a boil. Reduce the heat to low. Cook for 5 minutes or until the asparagus is tender-crisp.

2. Stir in the couscous. Cover the saucepan and remove from the heat. Let stand for 5 minutes. Fluff with a fork.

Vegetable-Rice Pilaf

MAKES: 4 SERVINGS

1	tablespoon butter
¾	cup uncooked regular long-grain white rice
1¾	cups Swanson® Vegetable Broth (Regular **or** Certified Organic)
¼	teaspoon dried basil leaves, crushed
¾	cup frozen mixed vegetables
¼	cup chopped green **or** red pepper

PREP: 5 MINUTES

COOK: 25 MINUTES

1. Heat the butter in a 2-quart saucepan over medium-high heat. Add the rice and cook for 30 seconds or until the rice is browned, stirring constantly.

2. Stir the broth and basil into the saucepan. Heat to a boil. Reduce the heat to low. Cover and cook for 10 minutes.

3. Stir in the vegetables and pepper. Cover and cook for 10 minutes more or until the rice is tender and most of the liquid is absorbed.

Cheeseburger Pasta

MAKES: 4 SERVINGS

PREP: 5 MINUTES

COOK: 20 MINUTES

1 pound ground beef

1 can (10¾ ounces) Campbell's® Condensed Cheddar Cheese Soup

1 can (10¾ ounces) Campbell's® Condensed Tomato Soup

1½ cups water

2 cups **uncooked** medium shell-shaped pasta

1. Cook the beef in a 10-inch skillet over medium-high heat until the beef is well browned, stirring frequently to break up meat. Pour off any fat.

2. Stir the soups, water and pasta into the skillet. Heat to a boil. Reduce the heat to medium. Cook for 10 minutes or until the pasta is tender but still firm, stirring often.

Mini Chocolate Cookie Cheesecakes

MAKES: 16 SERVINGS

PREP: 20 MINUTES

BAKE: 20 MINUTES

COOL: 1 HOUR

CHILL: 2 HOURS

**CAMPBELL'S
KITCHEN**

*For a refreshing flavor,
use the Pepperidge
Farm® Mini Mint
Milano® Cookies
instead of the regular
ones.*

16 foil baking cups (2½-inch)

2 packages (4.9 ounces **each**) Pepperidge Farm®
Mini Milano® Distinctive Cookies

2 packages (8 ounces **each**) cream cheese,
softened

½ cup sugar

2 eggs

½ teaspoon vanilla extract

1. Heat the oven to 350°F. Put the foil baking cups into
16 (2½-inch) muffin-pan cups or on a baking sheet. Place
2 cookies in the bottom of each cup and set aside. Cut the
remaining cookies in half.

2. Beat the cream cheese, sugar, eggs and vanilla in a
medium bowl with an electric mixer on medium speed
until smooth. Spoon the cheese mixture into the baking
cups filling each cup three-fourths full. Insert **2** cookie
halves, with the cut ends down, into the cheese mixture
of each cup.

3. Bake for 20 minutes or until the centers are set. Cool
the cheesecakes on a wire rack for 1 hour. Refrigerate the
cheesecakes for at least 2 hours before serving.

5 Ingredients or Less

You're just a few ingredients away from a delicious dish.

Sun-Dried Tomato Risotto

MAKES: 4 SERVINGS

PREP: 5 MINUTES

COOK: 25 MINUTES

STAND: 5 MINUTES

TIME-SAVING

To quickly thaw the peas, place them in a colander and run under warm water.

1	jar (8 ounces) oil-packed sun-dried tomato strips
1½	cups **uncooked** Arborio rice
4	cups Swanson® Chicken Broth (Regular, Natural Goodness™ **or** Certified Organic), **heated**
1	cup frozen peas, thawed
¼	cup walnuts, toasted and chopped

1. Drain **2 tablespoons** of oil from the tomatoes and set aside. Chop enough tomatoes to make ½ cup.

2. Heat the reserved oil in a 3-quart saucepan over medium heat. Add the tomatoes and rice and cook for 2 minutes or until the rice is opaque.

3. Stir **1 cup** of the hot broth into the rice mixture. Cook and stir until the broth is absorbed, maintaining the rice at a gentle simmer. Continue cooking and adding broth, ½ cup at a time, stirring until it's absorbed after each addition before adding more. Add the peas and walnuts with the last broth addition.

4. Remove the saucepan from the heat. Cover and let it stand for 5 minutes.

Parmesan Sun-Dried Tomato Risotto: Substitute grated Parmesan cheese for the walnuts.

Chicken Pesto with Tomatoes

MAKES: 4 SERVINGS

PREP: 5 MINUTES

COOK: 20 MINUTES

Vegetable cooking spray

4 skinless, boneless chicken breast halves

1 can (10¾ ounces) Campbell's® Condensed Cream of Chicken Soup (Regular **or** 98% Fat Free)

½ cup water

⅓ cup prepared pesto

1 can (14½ ounces) diced tomatoes, undrained

Hot cooked tube-shaped (penne) pasta (optional)

1. Spray a 10-inch skillet with cooking spray. Heat over medium-high heat for 1 minute. Add the chicken and cook for 10 minutes or until it's well browned on both sides. Remove the chicken.

2. Stir the soup, water, pesto and tomatoes into the skillet. Heat to a boil. Return the chicken to the skillet and reduce the heat to low. Cover and cook for 5 minutes or until the chicken is cooked through. Serve with pasta, if desired.

Pesto Crab Cakes

MAKES: 6 SERVINGS

PREP: 10 MINUTES

CHILL: 2 HOURS

BROIL: 10 MINUTES

CAMPBELL'S KITCHEN

Serve these crispy crab cakes with lemon wedges for a refreshing taste.

1 can (10¾ ounces) Campbell's® Condensed Cream of Celery Soup (Regular **or** 98% Fat Free)

⅓ cup prepared pesto

2 tablespoons drained, chopped pimiento

¼ cup plain dry bread crumbs

1 pound refrigerated pasteurized lump crabmeat

1. Stir together the soup, **2 tablespoons** of the pesto and pimiento. Add the bread crumbs and crabmeat and mix lightly. Cover and refrigerate for 2 hours.

2. Shape the mixture (using a ⅓ cup measuring cup) into 12 (about 1-inch-thick) patties and place on a rack in a broiler pan.

3. Heat the broiler. Broil the patties with the top of the patties about 6 inches from the source of heat for 10 to 12 minutes or until browned. Serve the crab cakes with the remaining pesto.

Tasty 2-Step Chicken

MAKES: 4 SERVINGS

PREP: 5 MINUTES

COOK: 20 MINUTES

1   tablespoon vegetable oil

4   skinless, boneless chicken breast halves

1   can (10¾ ounces) Campbell's® Condensed Cream of Mushroom Soup (Regular **or** 98% Fat Free)

½   cup water

1. Heat the oil in a 10-inch skillet over medium-high heat. Add the chicken and cook for 10 minutes until it's well browned on both sides. Remove the chicken and set aside. Pour off any fat.

2. Stir the soup and water into the skillet. Heat to a boil. Return the chicken to the skillet and reduce the heat to low. Cover and cook for 5 minutes or until the chicken is cooked through.

Butter-Glazed Asparagus

MAKES: 6 SERVINGS

½ cup Swanson® Broth (Chicken **or** Vegetable)

2 pounds asparagus, trimmed and cut into 1-inch pieces

6 tablespoons butter

PREP: 5 MINUTES

COOK: 10 MINUTES

1. Heat the broth in a 12-inch skillet over high heat to a boil. Add the asparagus and cook for 2 minutes. Add the butter.

2. Reduce the heat to medium. Cook for 5 minutes more or until the liquid thickens and the asparagus is tender-crisp.

EASY SUBSTITUTION

Use frozen broccoli flowerets or sliced carrots for the asparagus.

Power Breakfast Sandwiches

MAKES: 2 SANDWICHES

¼ cup peanut butter

4 slices Pepperidge Farm® Natural Whole Wheat Bread

¼ cup raisins

1 medium banana, sliced

PREP: 5 MINUTES

Spread the peanut butter on **4** of the bread slices. Divide the raisins and banana between **2** bread slices. Top with remaining bread slices, peanut butter-side down. Cut in half.

EASY SUBSTITUTION

Substitute 1 large apple, cored and sliced, for the raisins and banana.

Saucy Pork Chops

MAKES: 4 SERVINGS

PREP: 5 MINUTES

COOK: 20 MINUTES

1 tablespoon vegetable oil

4 pork chops, ½-inch thick

1 can (10¾ ounces) Campbell's® Condensed Cream of Onion Soup

¼ cup water

1. Heat the oil in a 10-inch skillet over medium-high heat. Add the pork chops and cook until they're well browned on both sides.

2. Stir the soup and water into the skillet. Heat to a boil. Reduce the heat to low. Cover and cook for 5 minutes or until the chops are cooked through.

Mini Turkey Meatballs Marinara

MAKES: 42 MEATBALLS

1   pound ground turkey

½   cup Pepperidge Farm® Herb Seasoned
      Stuffing, crushed

½   cup grated Parmesan cheese

1   egg, beaten
      Vegetable cooking spray

2¾ cups Prego® Marinara Italian Sauce

PREP: 25 MINUTES

COOK: 20 MINUTES

CAMPBELL'S
KITCHEN

This recipe can be an appetizer or served as a main dish with pasta.

1. Thoroughly mix the turkey, stuffing, cheese and egg in a large bowl. Shape the mixture into 42 (¾-inch) meatballs.

2. Spray a 12-inch nonstick skillet with cooking spray and heat over medium-high heat for 1 minute. Add the meatballs and cook in 2 batches or until they're well browned. Remove the meatballs with a slotted spoon and set aside.

3. Stir the sauce into the skillet. Heat to a boil. Return the meatballs to the skillet and reduce the heat to low. Cover and cook for 5 minutes or until the meatballs are cooked through.

Awesome Grilled Cheese Sandwiches

MAKES: 3 SANDWICHES

PREP: 10 MINUTES

COOK: 5 MINUTES

1 package (11.25 ounces) Pepperidge Farm® Frozen Garlic Texas Toast

6 slices fontina **or** fresh mozzarella cheese (about 6 ounces)

6 thin slices deli smoked turkey

3 thin slices prosciutto

1 jar (12 ounces) sliced roasted red peppers, drained

CAMPBELL'S KITCHEN

For a spicier flavor, add a dash of crushed red pepper flakes on the cheese when assembling the sandwiches.

1. Heat a panini or sandwich press according to the manufacturer's directions until hot. (Or use a cast-iron skillet or ridged grill pan.)

2. Top **3** of the bread slices with **half** of the cheese, turkey, proscuitto, peppers and remaining cheese. Top with the remaining bread slices.

3. Put the sandwiches on the press, closing the lid onto the sandwiches. Cook the sandwiches for 5 minutes (if cooking in a skillet or grill pan, press with a spatula occasionally or weigh down with another cast-iron skillet/foil-covered brick), until they're lightly browned and the bread is crisp and the cheese melts.

Chipotle Chili

PREP: 15 MINUTES

COOK: 8 TO 9 HOURS

1   jar (16 ounces) Pace® Chipotle **or** Regular Chunky Salsa

1   cup water

2   tablespoons chili powder

1   large onion, chopped (about 1 cup)

2   pounds beef for stew, cut into ½-inch pieces

1   can (about 19 ounces) red kidney beans, rinsed and drained

Shredded Cheddar cheese (optional)

Sour cream (optional)

1. Stir the salsa, water, chili powder, onion, beef and beans in a 3½-quart slow cooker.

2. Cover and cook on LOW for 8 to 9 hours* or until the meat is fork-tender. Serve with the cheese and sour cream, if desired.

*Or on HIGH for 4 to 5 hours

Creamy Blush Sauce with Turkey & Penne

MAKES: 8 SERVINGS

PREP: 10 MINUTES

COOK: 7 TO 8 HOURS,
10 MINUTES

**EASY
SUBSTITUTION**

*Substitute 8 bone-in
chicken thighs (about
2 pounds) for the
turkey thighs.
Makes 4 servings*

4	turkey thighs, skin removed (about 3 pounds)
2¾	cups Prego® Chunky Mushroom & Green Pepper Italian Sauce
½	teaspoon crushed red pepper
½	cup half-and-half
	Tube-shaped pasta (penne), cooked and drained
	Grated Parmesan cheese

1. Put the turkey in a 3½- to 5-quart slow cooker. Pour the sauce over the turkey and sprinkle with the red pepper.

2. Cover and cook on LOW for 7 to 8 hours* or until the turkey is fork-tender and cooked through. Remove the turkey from the cooker with a fork or tongs to a cutting board. Remove the turkey meat from the bones.

3. Stir the turkey meat and the half-and-half into the cooker. Cover and cook for 10 minutes or until hot. Spoon the sauce and turkey over the pasta. Sprinkle with the cheese.

Or on HIGH for 4 to 5 hours

French Onion Burgers

MAKES: 4 BURGERS

PREP: 5 MINUTES

COOK: 20 MINUTES

1 pound ground beef

1 can (10½ ounces) Campbell's® Condensed French Onion Soup

4 slices cheese

4 round hard rolls, split

1. Shape the beef into 4 (½-inch-thick) burgers.

2. Heat a 10-inch skillet over medium-high heat. Add the burgers and cook until they're well browned on both sides. Remove the burgers and set aside. Pour off any fat.

3. Stir the soup into the skillet. Heat to a boil. Return the burgers to the skillet and reduce the heat to low. Cover and cook for 5 minutes or until the burgers are cooked through. Top with the cheese and continue cooking until the cheese melts. Serve burgers in rolls with soup mixture for dipping.

Game-Winning Drumsticks

MAKES: ABOUT 6 SERVINGS

PREP: 10 MINUTES

MARINATE: 4 HOURS

BAKE: 1 HOUR

CAMPBELL'S
KITCHEN

Keep disposable aluminum foil baking pans on hand to tote casseroles to friends' parties or covered dish suppers and for transporting. As a safety reminder, be sure to support the bottom of the filled pan when handling them in and out of the oven.

12   chicken drumsticks (about 4 pounds)

1¾   cups Swanson® Chicken Broth (Regular, Natural Goodness™ **or** Certified Organic)

½   cup Dijon mustard

⅓   cup Italian-seasoned dry bread crumbs

1. Put the chicken in a single layer in a 15×10-inch disposable aluminum foil bakeware pan.

2. Stir the broth and mustard in a small bowl. Pour the broth mixture over the chicken and turn to coat. Sprinkle the bread crumbs over the chicken. Refrigerate for 4 hours.

3. Bake at 375°F. for 1 hour or until the chicken is cooked through. Serve immediately or let stand for 30 minutes to serve at room temperature, using the pan juices as a dipping sauce.

Garlic Mashed Potatoes & Beef Bake

MAKES: 4 SERVINGS

PREP: 10 MINUTES

BAKE: 20 MINUTES

1 pound ground beef

1 can (10¾ ounces) Campbell's® Condensed Cream of Mushroom with Roasted Garlic Soup

1 tablespoon Worcestershire sauce

1 bag (16 ounces) frozen vegetable combination (broccoli, cauliflower, carrots), thawed

1 container (1 pound 10 ounces) refrigerated prepared mashed potatoes

1. Cook the beef in a 10-inch skillet over medium-high heat until the beef is well browned, stirring frequently to break up meat. Pour off any fat.

2. Stir the beef, ½ **can** of the soup, Worcestershire and vegetables in an 11×8-inch (2-quart) shallow baking dish.

3. Stir the remaining soup and the potatoes in a small bowl and spoon over the beef mixture.

4. Bake at 400°F. for 20 minutes or until hot.

Ultra Creamy Mashed Potatoes

MAKES: 6 SERVINGS

3½ cups Swanson® Chicken Broth (Regular,
   Natural Goodness™ **or** Certified Organic)

5 large potatoes, cut into 1-inch pieces (about
   7½ cups)

½ cup light cream

2 tablespoons butter

   Generous dash ground black pepper (optional)

PREP: 5 MINUTES

COOK: 20 MINUTES

1. Heat the broth and potatoes in a 3-quart saucepan over medium-high heat to a boil.

2. Reduce the heat to medium. Cover and cook for 10 minutes or until the potatoes are tender. Drain, reserving the broth.

3. Mash the potatoes with **¼ cup** broth, cream, butter and black pepper, if desired. Add additional broth, if needed, until desired consistency.

Ultimate Mashed Potatoes: Stir *½ cup sour cream*, *3 slices bacon*, cooked and crumbled (reserve some for garnish), and *¼ cup chopped fresh chives* into hot mashed potatoes. Sprinkle with remaining bacon.

Grilled Beef Steak with Sautéed Onions

MAKES: 8 SERVINGS

PREP: 5 MINUTES

COOK: 25 MINUTES

2   tablespoons olive oil

2   large onions, thinly sliced (about 2 cups)

2   pounds boneless beef sirloin, strip **or** rib steaks, cut into 8 pieces

1   jar (16 ounces) Pace® Chunky Salsa

1. Heat **1 tablespoon** of the oil in a 12-inch skillet over medium heat. Add the onions and cook until they're tender. Remove the onions from the skillet and keep warm.

2. Heat the remaining oil in the skillet. Add the steak pieces and cook until they're well browned on both sides.

3. Add the salsa and return the onions to the skillet. Cook for 3 minutes for medium-rare or until desired doneness.

Frosty Fruit Cooler

MAKES: 2 SERVINGS

PREP: 10 MINUTES

1 cup V8 Splash® Orange Pineapple **or**
   V8 Splash® Tropical Blend Juice Drink

¼ cup vanilla yogurt

½ cup cut-up strawberries **or** raspberries

½ cup ice cubes

Put the juice, yogurt, strawberries and ice in an electric blender container. Cover and blend until smooth. Serve immediately.

Shredded Chicken Soft Tacos

MAKES: 8 TACOS

PREP: 5 MINUTES

COOK: 10 MINUTES

TIME-SAVING

Use store-bought rotisserie chicken or refrigerated cooked chicken strips.

1 jar (16 ounces) Pace® Picante Sauce

3 cups shredded cooked chicken

8 flour tortillas (8-inch), warmed

  Guacamole

  Chopped tomatoes

  Fresh cilantro sprigs (optional)

1. Heat the sauce and chicken in a 2-quart saucepan over medium heat until the mixture is hot and bubbling, stirring often.

2. Spoon about ⅓ **cup** of the chicken mixture down the center of each tortilla. Top with the guacamole, tomatoes and cilantro, if desired. Fold the tortilla around the filling.

Frosty Fruit Cooler

Ham & Broccoli Shortcut Stromboli

MAKES: 4 SERVINGS

PREP: 10 MINUTES

BAKE: 20 MINUTES

Vegetable cooking spray

1   package (10 ounces) refrigerated pizza dough

1   can (10¾ ounces) Campbell's® Condensed Cream of Celery Soup (Regular **or** 98% Fat Free)

1   cup chopped broccoli, cooked and drained

2   cups cubed cooked ham

1   cup shredded Cheddar cheese (4 ounces)

CAMPBELL'S KITCHEN

You will need at least 8 ounces boneless cooked ham for the amount needed for this recipe.

1. Heat the oven to 400°F. Spray a baking sheet with cooking spray. Unroll the dough onto the prepared sheet.

2. Stir the soup, broccoli and ham in a small bowl. Spread the soup mixture down the center of the dough. Top with the cheese. Fold the long sides of the dough over filling and pinch the edges to seal. Turn over and place seam-side down. Cut several 2-inch-long slits in top of dough.

3. Bake for 20 minutes or until golden.

Asparagus & Bacon Potatoes

MAKES: 4 SERVINGS

1 can (10¾ ounces) Campbell's® Condensed
    Cream of Asparagus Soup

4 hot baked potatoes, split

9 slices bacon, cooked and crumbled
    Shredded Cheddar or Swiss cheese (optional)

PREP: 15 MINUTES

BAKE: 5 MINUTES

CAMPBELL'S
KITCHEN

1. Stir the soup in the can until it's smooth.

2. Place the potatoes on a baking sheet. Fluff the potatoes with a fork. Top with the bacon.

3. Spoon the soup over the potatoes. Top with cheese, if desired. Bake at 400°F. for 5 minutes or until the soup is hot.

You can either bake the potatoes in an oven or use the microwave. First, pierce the potatoes with a fork. Bake at 400°F. for 1 hour or microwave on HIGH for 10½ to 12½ minutes or until they're fork-tender.

I'm Dreamy for a White Chocolate Fondue

MAKES: 1½ CUPS

PREP: 5 MINUTES

BAKE: 10 MINUTES

⅓ cup heavy cream

1 tablespoon orange-flavored liqueur **or** ½ teaspoon orange extract

1 package (about 12 ounces) white chocolate pieces

Suggested Dippers: Assorted Pepperidge Farm® Cookies, whole strawberries, banana chunks, dried pineapple pieces **and/or** fresh pineapple chunks

1. Stir the cream, liqueur and chocolate in a 1-quart saucepan. Heat over low heat until the chocolate melts, stirring occasionally.

2. Pour the chocolate mixture into a fondue pot or slow cooker.

3. Serve warm with the ***Suggested Dippers***.

Quick Skillet & Casserole Meals

From stove to table with minimal fuss—it's so easy.

Halibut with Beans and Spinach

MAKES: 4 SERVINGS

PREP: 10 MINUTES

COOK: 15 MINUTES

2 tablespoons olive oil

1 teaspoon minced garlic

4 (6 ounces **each**) fresh halibut fillets

1¾ cups Swanson® Chicken Broth (Regular, Natural Goodness™ **or** Certified Organic)

2 tablespoons lemon juice

2 cups frozen cut leaf spinach

1 can (about 15 ounces) Great Northern beans, rinsed and drained

Generous dash crushed red pepper

1. Stir **1 tablespoon** of the oil and garlic in a shallow dish. Add the halibut and turn to coat.

2. Heat the remaining oil in a 10-inch skillet over medium-high heat. Add the fish and cook for about 4 minutes, turning halfway through cooking. Remove the fish with a spatula.

3. Stir the broth and lemon juice into the skillet. Heat to a boil. Add the spinach, beans and red pepper. Return the fish to the skillet. Reduce the heat to low. Cover and cook for 2 minutes or until the fish flakes easily when tested with a fork and the mixture is hot and bubbling.

Lemon Chicken Tarragon

MAKES: 4 SERVINGS

PREP: 5 MINUTES

COOK: 20 MINUTES

1 tablespoon olive **or** vegetable oil

4 skinless, boneless chicken breast halves

2 cups water

1 can (10¾ ounces) Campbell's® Condensed Cream of Chicken Soup (Regular **or** 98% Fat Free)

2 tablespoons lemon juice

1 tablespoon finely chopped fresh tarragon **or** 1 teaspoon dried tarragon leaves, crushed

⅛ teaspoon ground black pepper

2 cups **uncooked** instant white rice

1. Heat the oil in a 12-inch skillet over medium-high heat. Add the chicken and cook for 10 minutes or until it's well browned on both sides. Remove the chicken.

2. Stir the water, soup, lemon juice, tarragon and black pepper into the skillet. Heat to a boil.

3. Stir in the rice. Return the chicken to the skillet and reduce the heat to low. Cover and cook for 5 minutes or until the chicken is cooked through and the rice is tender.

Pork Diane

MAKES: 4 SERVINGS

PREP: 5 MINUTES

COOK: 20 MINUTES

4   boneless pork chops

1   tablespoon vegetable oil

1   small sweet onion, chopped (about ¼ cup)

2   cloves garlic, minced

¼   cup brandy

1   can (10¾ ounces) Campbell's® Condensed Tomato Soup

½   cup Swanson® Chicken Broth (Regular, Natural Goodness™ **or** Certified Organic)

2   teaspoons Worcestershire sauce

1   teaspoon coarse-grain mustard

     Roasted potatoes

EASY SUBSTITUTION

Instead of the brandy, you may increase the broth to ¾ cup.

1. Season the pork chops as desired.

2. Heat the oil in a 10-inch skillet over medium-high heat. Add the pork chops and cook until browned on both sides. Remove the chops.

3. Add the onion and cook until tender. Add the garlic and cook for 30 seconds.

4. Stir the brandy into the skillet. Heat to a boil and cook until the liquid is reduced by half. Stir the soup, broth, Worcestershire sauce and mustard into the skillet. Heat to a boil. Return the chops to the skillet and reduce the heat to low. Cook for 15 minutes or until the pork is cooked through. Serve with roasted potatoes.

Quick Creamy Chicken & Corn

MAKES: 4 SERVINGS

PREP: 15 MINUTES

COOK: 25 MINUTES

1   tablespoon vegetable oil

4   skinless, boneless chicken breast halves

1   can (10¾ ounces) Campbell's® Condensed Cream of Chicken Soup (Regular **or** 98% Fat Free)

¾   cup water

½   teaspoon poultry seasoning

1   package (10 ounces) frozen whole kernel corn

2   cups refrigerated cubed potatoes

2   tablespoons chopped fresh parsley

1   cup shredded Cheddar cheese (4 ounces)

1. Heat the oil in a 10-inch skillet over medium-high heat. Add the chicken and cook for 10 minutes or until it's well browned on both sides.

2. Stir the soup, water, poultry seasoning, corn and potatoes into the skillet. Heat to a boil. Reduce the heat to low. Cover and cook for 10 minutes or until the chicken is cooked through. Stir in the parsley and sprinkle with the cheese.

Savory Mushroom Bread Pudding

MAKES: 6 SERVINGS

PREP: 5 MINUTES

STAND: 30 MINUTES

BAKE: 45 MINUTES

Vegetable cooking spray

12 slices Pepperidge Farm® White **or** Whole Wheat Bread, cut into cubes

1 package (8 ounces) sliced mushrooms

1 can (10¾ ounces) Campbell's® Condensed Cream of Mushroom Soup (Regular **or** 98% Fat Free)

4 eggs

2½ cups milk

1 teaspoon dried thyme leaves, crushed

⅛ teaspoon ground black pepper

1 cup shredded Swiss cheese (4 ounces)

1. Heat the oven to 375°F. Spray a 13×9-inch (3-quart) shallow baking dish with cooking spray.

2. Add the bread and mushrooms to prepared baking dish.

3. Beat the soup, eggs, milk, thyme and black pepper with a whisk or a fork in a medium bowl. Pour over the bread and mushrooms, pressing down the bread to coat. Let stand for 30 minutes.

4. Bake for 35 minutes. Top with the cheese. Bake for 10 minutes more or until the cheese melts.

Skillet Vegetable Lasagna

MAKES: 4 SERVINGS

PREP: 10 MINUTES

COOK: 15 MINUTES

1¾ cups Swanson® Vegetable Broth (Regular **or** Certified Organic)

10 **uncooked** oven-ready (no-boil) lasagna noodles

1 can (10¾ ounces) Campbell's® Condensed Cream of Mushroom Soup (Regular **or** 98% Fat Free)

1 can (14.5 ounces) diced canned tomatoes, undrained

1 package (10 ounces) frozen chopped spinach, thawed

1 cup ricotta cheese

1 cup shredded mozzarella cheese (4 ounces)

1. Heat the broth in a 12-inch skillet over medium-high heat to a boil. Break up the noodles into pieces and add to the broth. Reduce the heat to low. Cook for about 3 minutes or until the noodles are tender but still firm.

2. Stir the soup, tomatoes and spinach into the skillet. Cook for about 5 minutes or until the mixture is hot and bubbling.

3. Remove the skillet from the heat. Spoon the ricotta cheese on top and sprinkle with the mozzarella cheese.

Spicy Chicken & Chorizo

MAKES: 4 SERVINGS

PREP: 15 MINUTES

COOK: 20 MINUTES

1 tablespoon vegetable oil

2 stalks celery, chopped (about 1 cup)

1 medium red pepper, diced (about 1 cup)

2 cups Swanson® Chicken Broth (Regular, Natural Goodness™ **or** Certified Organic)

1 can (about 4 ounces) Pace™ Diced Green Chiles

2 tablespoons tomato paste

2 cups refrigerated cooked chicken strips

2 cups **uncooked** instant white rice

4 ounces chorizo sausage, crumbled (about ½ cup)

¼ cup chopped fresh cilantro

Hot pepper sauce (optional)

1. Heat the oil in a 10-inch skillet over medium-high heat. Add the celery and red pepper. Cook for about 3 minutes or until tender.

2. Stir the broth, chiles and tomato paste into the skillet. Heat to a boil. Reduce the heat to low. Add the chicken, rice and sausage. Cover and cook for about 10 minutes or until the rice is tender. Stir in the cilantro. Serve with hot pepper sauce, if desired.

Zucchini & Chicken Rice Casserole

MAKES: 4 SERVINGS

PREP: 10 MINUTES

BAKE: 35 MINUTES

STAND: 10 MINUTES

Vegetable cooking spray

1 package (12 ounces) breaded cooked chicken tenders, cut into bite-sized strips

2 large zucchini, cut in half lengthwise and thinly sliced (about 4 cups)

1 jar (7 ounces) whole roasted sweet peppers, drained and thinly sliced

1 cup **uncooked** quick-cooking brown rice

1 can (10¾ ounces) Campbell's® Condensed Cream of Celery Soup (Regular **or** 98% Fat Free)

1 soup can water

½ cup sour cream

1. Heat the oven to 375°F. Spray a 13×9-inch (3-quart) shallow baking dish with cooking spray.

2. Stir the chicken, zucchini, peppers and rice in the prepared dish.

3. Stir the soup, water and sour cream with a spoon in a small bowl. Pour over the chicken mixture. **Cover**.

4. Bake for 35 minutes or until the rice is tender. Let the casserole stand for 10 minutes before serving. Stir the rice.

Creamy Provençal Vegetable Stew

MAKES: 4 SERVINGS

PREP: 10 MINUTES

COOK: 15 MINUTES

CAMPBELL'S
KITCHEN

*For a meatless recipe,
substitute Campbell's®
Cream of Mushroom
Soup for the chicken
soup and use
Swanson® Vegetable
Broth for the chicken
broth.*

2   tablespoons olive oil

1   small eggplant, cut into cubes (about 3 cups)

1   cup sliced mushrooms

1   medium onion, chopped (about ½ cup)

2   cloves garlic, minced

1   can (10¾ ounces) Campbell's® Condensed
     Cream of Chicken Soup (Regular **or** 98% Fat
     Free)

1   cup Swanson® Chicken Broth (Regular, Natural
     Goodness™ **or** Certified Organic)

1   can (14.5 ounces) diced tomatoes, undrained

½   teaspoon dried thyme leaves, crushed

1. Heat the oil in a 10-inch skillet over medium heat. Add the eggplant, mushrooms, onion and garlic and cook until tender.

2. Stir the soup, broth, tomatoes and thyme into the skillet. Heat to a boil. Reduce the heat to low. Cook for 5 minutes or until the flavors are blended.

Greek Rice Bake

MAKES: 6 SERVINGS

PREP: 10 MINUTES

COOK: 45 MINUTES

STAND: 5 MINUTES

1   can (10¾ ounces) Campbell's® Condensed Cream of Mushroom Soup (Regular **or** 98% Fat Free)

½   cup water

1   can (about 15 ounces) diced tomatoes, undrained

1   jar (6 ounces) marinated artichoke hearts, drained and cut in half

2   portobello mushrooms, coarsely chopped (about 2 cups)

¾   cup **uncooked** quick-cooking brown rice

1   can (about 15 ounces) small white beans, rinsed and drained

3   to 4 tablespoons crumbled feta cheese

1. Stir the soup, water, tomatoes, artichokes, mushrooms, rice and beans in a 2-quart casserole. **Cover**.

2. Bake at 400°F. for 40 minutes or until the rice is tender. Stir.

3. Let the casserole stand for 5 minutes and sprinkle with the cheese before serving.

Mixed Berry Strata

MAKES: 4 SERVINGS

PREP: 10 MINUTES

CHILL: 2 HOURS

BAKE: 40 MINUTES

STAND: 5 MINUTES

CAMPBELL'S KITCHEN

For easy cleanup, spray the baking dish with vegetable cooking spray.

5   slices Pepperidge Farm® Toasting White Bread, torn into 1-inch pieces

4   eggs

1   cup milk

¼   cup orange juice

½   cup ricotta cheese

¼   cup sugar

2   tablespoons butter, melted

1   bag (12 ounces) frozen mixed berries (strawberries, blueberries, raspberries), thawed and drained

Confectioners' sugar (optional)

1. Put the bread in an 11×8-inch (2-quart) shallow baking dish.

2. Beat the eggs, milk, orange juice, cheese, sugar and butter with a whisk or fork in a medium bowl. Stir in the berries. Pour the egg mixture over the bread. Cover and refrigerate for 2 hours or overnight.

3. Uncover the dish. Bake at 350°F. for 40 minutes or until a knife inserted near the center comes out clean. Let the strata stand for 5 minutes before serving. Sprinkle with confectioners' sugar, if desired.

Savory Orange Chicken with Sage

MAKES: 4 SERVINGS

PREP: 10 MINUTES

COOK: 20 MINUTES

4   skinless, boneless chicken breast halves

½   cup all-purpose flour

1   tablespoon vegetable oil

1   tablespoon butter

1¾   cups Swanson® Chicken Broth (Regular, Natural Goodness™ **or** Certified Organic)

⅓   cup orange juice

¼   cup Chablis **or** other dry white wine

1   tablespoon grated orange peel

1   tablespoon chopped fresh sage leaves **or** 1 teaspoon ground sage

1   container (3.5 ounces) shiitake mushrooms, chopped (about 2 cups)

Hot cooked rice

1. Coat the chicken with the flour.

2. Heat the oil and butter in a 12-inch skillet over medium-high heat. Add the chicken and cook for 10 minutes or until it's well browned on both sides. Remove the chicken and set aside.

3. Stir the broth, juice, wine, peel and sage into the skillet. Heat to a boil.

4. Add the mushrooms. Return the chicken to the skillet and reduce the heat to low. Cook for 5 minutes or until the chicken is cooked through and liquid has reduced by one-fourth. Serve with rice.

Mozzarella Zucchini Skillet

MAKES: 7 SERVINGS

PREP: 10 MINUTES

COOK: 15 MINUTES

2 tablespoons vegetable oil

5 medium zucchini, sliced (about 7½ cups)

1 medium onion, chopped (about ½ cup)

¼ teaspoon garlic powder **or** 2 cloves garlic, minced

1½ cups Prego® Traditional Italian Sauce

½ cup shredded mozzarella **or** Cheddar cheese

1. Heat the oil in a 12-inch skillet over medium-high heat. Add the zucchini, onion and garlic powder and cook until the vegetables are tender-crisp.

2. Stir the sauce into the skillet and heat through.

3. Sprinkle with the cheese. Cover and cook until the cheese melts.

Chicken & Roasted Garlic Risotto

MAKES: 4 SERVINGS

PREP: 5 MINUTES

COOK: 20 MINUTES

STAND: 5 MINUTES

4   skinless, boneless chicken breast halves

1   tablespoon butter

1   can (10¾ ounces) Campbell's® Condensed Cream of Chicken Soup (Regular **or** 98% Fat Free)

1   can (10¾ ounces) Campbell's® Condensed Cream of Mushroom with Roasted Garlic Soup

2   cups water

2   cups **uncooked** instant white rice

1   cup frozen peas and carrots

1. Season the chicken as desired.

2. Heat the butter in a 10-inch skillet over medium-high heat. Add the chicken and cook for 10 minutes or until it's well browned on both sides. Remove the chicken and set aside.

3. Stir the soups and water into the skillet. Heat to a boil. Stir in the rice and vegetables. Return the chicken to the skillet and reduce the heat to low. Cover and cook for 5 minutes or until the chicken is cooked through. Remove from the heat. Let stand for 5 minutes.

Seafood Imperial

MAKES: 4 SERVINGS

PREP: 5 MINUTES

COOK: 10 MINUTES

2   tablespoons butter

2   green onions, chopped (about ¼ cup)

1   container (8 ounces) refrigerated pasteurized crabmeat, drained

8   ounces cooked shrimp, chopped

1   teaspoon seafood seasoning

1   can (10¾ ounces) Campbell's® Condensed Cream of Celery Soup (Regular **or** 98% Fat Free)

1   cup shredded white Cheddar cheese (4 ounces)

2   tablespoons mayonnaise

4   slices Pepperidge Farm® Bread, toasted and cut in half

1. Heat the butter in a 12-inch skillet over medium heat. Add the green onions and cook until tender. Stir in the crabmeat, shrimp and seafood seasoning and toss to coat.

2. Stir the soup into the skillet. Heat to a boil. Cook until the mixture is hot and bubbling.

3. Add the cheese and mayonnaise. Cook until the cheese melts, stirring occasionally.

4. Divide the crabmeat mixture over the toast. Sprinkle with additional green onions and cheese, if desired.

Savory Skillet Chicken & Rice

MAKES: 4 SERVINGS

1 tablespoon butter

1 pound skinless, boneless chicken breasts, cut into cubes

1 can (10¾ ounces) Campbell's® Condensed Cream of Mushroom Soup (Regular **or** 98% Fat Free)

1 cup milk

1 tablespoon onion flakes

¼ teaspoon dried thyme leaves, crushed

⅛ teaspoon ground black pepper

1 can (about 16 ounces) cut green beans, drained

2 cups **uncooked** instant white rice

PREP: 5 MINUTES

COOK: 20 MINUTES

STAND: 5 MINUTES

1. Heat the butter in a 10-inch skillet over medium-high heat. Add the chicken and cook until it's well browned, stirring often.

2. Stir the soup, milk, onion, thyme and black pepper into the skillet. Heat to a boil. Reduce the heat to low. Cover and cook for 5 minutes or until chicken is cooked through.

3. Stir in the beans and rice. Cover the skillet and remove from the heat. Let stand for 5 minutes. Fluff the rice with a fork.

10-Minute Prep

Minimal prep—maximum results

Easy One-Pot Spaghetti & Clams

MAKES: 6 SERVINGS

PREP: 5 MINUTES

COOK: 20 MINUTES

3 tablespoons olive oil

3 cloves garlic, minced

¼ teaspoon crushed red pepper flakes (optional)

8 cups Swanson® Chicken Broth (Regular, Natural Goodness™ **or** Certified Organic)

1 can (6.5 ounces) chopped clams, undrained

1 package (16 ounces) **uncooked** thin spaghetti

1 can (10 ounces) whole baby clams, undrained

18 littleneck clams, scrubbed

⅓ cup chopped fresh parsley

CAMPBELL'S KITCHEN

When using fresh clams, the shells should be tightly closed. If the shells are open, tap them slightly, and if they don't close shut, the clam is no longer alive and should be discarded. Also, after cooking discard any clams that do not open.

1. Heat the oil in a 4-quart saucepan over medium heat. Add the garlic and red pepper, if desired. Cook for 1 minute. Add the broth and chopped clams. Heat to a boil.

2. Add the spaghetti. Cook for about 9 minutes or until the broth is absorbed. Add the canned and fresh clams. Cook for 2 minutes or until the fresh clams open. Toss with the parsley.

Chili Pulled Beef Sandwiches

MAKES: 8 SANDWICHES

PREP: 5 MINUTES

COOK: 6 TO 8 HOURS

STAND: 10 MINUTES

2-pound boneless beef chuck roast

1 tablespoon barbecue seasoning

1 can (19 ounces) Campbell's® Chunky Grilled Steak Chili with Beans

1 large onion, thinly sliced (about 1 cup)

1 package (14 ounces) Pepperidge Farm® Hot Dog Buns

½ cup shredded Colby Jack cheese

1. Coat the roast with the seasoning.

2. Stir the chili and onion in a 5-quart slow cooker. Add the roast and turn to coat.

3. Cover and cook on LOW for 6 to 8 hours* or until the roast is fork-tender.

4. Remove the roast from the cooker to a cutting board and let it stand for 10 minutes. Shred the meat using 2 forks and return the meat to the cooker. Serve on the rolls with the cheese.

Or on HIGH for 3 to 4 hours

Turkey & Tortellini Alfredo

MAKES: 6 SERVINGS

PREP: 5 MINUTES

COOK: 15 MINUTES

1   pound Italian-style turkey sausage, casing removed

1   can (10¾ ounces) Campbell's® Condensed Cream of Chicken Soup (Regular **or** 98% Fat Free)

½   cup water

1   can (14.5 ounces) diced tomatoes, undrained

1   pound frozen cheese-filled tortellini

2   tablespoons chopped fresh basil

Grated Parmesan cheese (optional)

1. Cook the sausage in a 10-inch skillet over medium-high heat until it's well browned, stirring frequently to break up meat.

2. Stir the soup, water and tomatoes into the skillet. Heat to a boil. Add the tortellini and reduce the heat to low. Cook for about 5 minutes or until the tortellini is tender but still firm.

3. Stir in the basil. Serve with cheese, if desired.

Creamy Tuscan Bean & Chicken Soup

MAKES: 4 TO 6 SERVINGS

PREP: 10 MINUTES

COOK: 10 MINUTES

CAMPBELL'S KITCHEN

For shredded chicken, purchase a rotisserie chicken. Remove the skin and bones. You can either shred the chicken with your fingers or use 2 forks.

2   cans (10¾ ounces **each**) Campbell's® Condensed Cream of Celery Soup (Regular **or** 98% Fat Free)

2   cups water

1   can (about 15 ounces) white kidney (cannellini) beans, rinsed and drained

1   can (14.5 ounces) diced tomatoes, undrained

2   cups diced **or** shredded cooked chicken

¼   cup bacon bits

3   ounces fresh baby spinach leaves

     Olive oil

     Grated Parmesan cheese

1. Heat the soup, water, beans, tomatoes, chicken and bacon in a 3-quart saucepan over medium-high heat to a boil.

2. Add the spinach. Cook for 5 minutes or until the spinach wilts.

3. Serve the soup with a drizzle of oil and sprinkle with cheese.

Bistro-Style Short Ribs

MAKES: 4 SERVINGS

PREP: 10 MINUTES

COOK: 15 MINUTES

BAKE: 1 HOUR 30 MINUTES

Vegetable cooking spray

3   pounds beef short ribs, cut into individual rib pieces

1   large onion, chopped (about 1 cup)

2   medium carrots, chopped (about ⅔ cup)

1   stalk celery, chopped (about ½ cup)

2¾ cups Prego® Traditional Italian Sauce

1¾ cups Swanson® Beef Broth (Regular, Lower Sodium **or** Certified Organic)

1. Spray an oven-safe 6-quart saucepot with cooking spray. Heat over medium-high heat for 1 minute. Cook the ribs in 2 batches or until they're browned on all sides. Remove the ribs with a slotted spoon and set aside. Pour off all but 2 tablespoons fat.

2. Add the onion, carrots and celery and cook until tender. Stir the sauce and broth into the saucepot. Heat to a boil. Return the ribs to the pot. Cover and bake at 350°F. for 1 hour 30 minutes or until the meat is fork-tender. Remove the ribs with a fork or kitchen tongs. Spoon off any fat from the sauce.

Slow-Cooked Bistro-Style Ribs: Brown the ribs in a 12-inch skillet as directed in step 1. Place the onion, carrots and celery in a 3½- to 6-quart slow cooker. Top with the ribs. Stir the sauce and broth into the cooker. Cover and cook on LOW for 7 to 8 hours* or until the meat is fork-tender. Remove the ribs with a fork or kitchen tongs from the cooker. Spoon off any fat from the sauce.

Or on HIGH for 3½ to 4 hours

Fresh Tomato Basil Chicken

MAKES: 4 SERVINGS

PREP: 5 MINUTES

COOK: 20 MINUTES

1 tablespoon vegetable oil

4 skinless, boneless chicken breast halves

1 can (10¾ ounces) Campbell's® Condensed Cream of Mushroom Soup (Regular **or** 98% Fat Free)

⅓ cup water

1 tablespoon chopped fresh parsley

1 tablespoon chopped fresh basil

½ cup chopped plum tomato

1 tablespoon butter

1. Heat the oil in a 10-inch skillet over medium-high heat. Add the chicken and cook for 10 minutes or until it's well browned on both sides.

2. Stir the soup, water, parsley, basil and tomato into the skillet. Heat to a boil. Reduce the heat to low. Cover and cook for 5 minutes or until the chicken is cooked through. Stir in the butter just before serving.

Herb Roasted Chicken & Vegetables

MAKES: 4 SERVINGS

PREP: 10 MINUTES

BAKE: 50 MINUTES

CAMPBELL'S KITCHEN

Consider substituting white wine for the water and you can create a simply elegant dish perfect for company.

1 can (10¾ ounces) Campbell's® Condensed Cream of Mushroom Soup (Regular **or** 98% Fat Free)

⅓ cup water

2 teaspoons dried oregano leaves, crushed

4 medium potatoes, cut into quarters

2 cups fresh **or** frozen baby whole carrots

4 bone-in chicken breast halves

½ teaspoon paprika

1. Stir the soup, water, **1 teaspoon** of the oregano, potatoes and carrots in a roasting pan.

2. Top with the chicken. Sprinkle with the remaining oregano and paprika.

3. Bake at 400°F. for 50 minutes or until the chicken is cooked through. Stir the vegetables.

Pacific Coast Salmon
with Pan-Roasted Corn Salsa

MAKES: 4 SERVINGS

PREP: 5 MINUTES

BAKE: 15 MINUTES

COOK: 8 MINUTES

4   fresh salmon fillets (about 1½ pounds)

1   jar (16 ounces) Pace® Chunky Salsa

1   teaspoon olive oil

1   cup frozen whole kernel corn, thawed

1   tablespoon chopped fresh cilantro

1   tablespoon lemon juice

1. Put the salmon in a roasting pan. Spoon ½ **cup** of the salsa over the fish.

2. Bake at 400°F. for 15 minutes or until the fish flakes easily when tested with a fork.

3. Heat the oil in an 8-inch skillet over medium heat. Add the corn and cook for 4 minutes or until the corn starts to brown.

4. Stir the remaining salsa, cilantro and lemon juice into the skillet and heat through. Serve the salmon with the corn salsa.

Turkey and Stuffing Casserole

MAKES: 6 SERVINGS

PREP: 5 MINUTES

BAKE: 25 MINUTES

Vegetable cooking spray

1   can (10¾ ounces) Campbell's® Condensed Cream of Mushroom Soup (Regular **or** 98% Fat Free)

1   cup milk **or** water

1   bag (16 ounces) frozen vegetable combination (broccoli, cauliflower, carrots), thawed

2   cups cubed cooked turkey **or** chicken

4   cups Pepperidge Farm® Cubed Herb Seasoned Stuffing

1   cup shredded Swiss **or** Cheddar cheese (4 ounces)

EASY SUBSTITUTION

When you don't have any leftover turkey or chicken for this recipe, substitute 1 can (9.75 ounces) Swanson® Premium White Chunk Chicken Breast, drained.

1. Spray an 11×8-inch (2-quart) shallow baking dish with cooking spray and set aside.

2. Stir the soup and milk in a large bowl. Stir in the vegetables, turkey and stuffing. Spoon the mixture into the prepared dish.

3. Bake at 400°F. for 20 minutes or until hot and bubbly. Stir.

4. Sprinkle the cheese over the turkey mixture. Bake for 5 minutes more or until the cheese melts.

Pennsylvania Dutch Ham & Noodle Casserole

MAKES: 4 SERVINGS

PREP: 10 MINUTES

COOK: 15 MINUTES

CAMPBELL'S
KITCHEN

Substitute cooked chicken or turkey for ham.

1   tablespoon vegetable oil

2   cups cubed cooked ham (about 1 pound)

1   medium onion, chopped (about ½ cup)

1   can (10¾ ounces) Campbell's® Condensed Cream of Mushroom Soup (Regular **or** 98% Fat Free)

8   ounces extra-sharp Cheddar cheese

8   ounces extra-wide egg noodles, cooked and drained

1. Heat the oil in a 4-quart saucepan over medium-high heat. Add the ham and onion and cook until the onion is tender.

2. Stir the soup into the saucepan. Heat to a boil. Reduce the heat to low. Add the cheese and stir until the cheese melts. Add the noodles and heat through.

Shredded BBQ Chicken Sandwiches

MAKES: 8 SANDWICHES

PREP: 5 MINUTES

COOK: 25 MINUTES

2   jars (16 ounces **each**) Pace® Chunky Salsa

1   tablespoon apple cider vinegar

¼   cup packed brown sugar

½   teaspoon garlic powder

¼   teaspoon chili powder

1   pound skinless, boneless chicken breast halves

1   package (13 ounces) Pepperidge Farm®
    Sandwich Buns
    Shredded Cheddar cheese

1. Heat the salsa, vinegar, brown sugar, garlic powder and chili powder in a 3-quart saucepan over medium-high heat to a boil.

2. Add the chicken to the saucepan and reduce the heat to low. Cover and cook for 20 minutes or until the chicken is cooked through.

3. Remove the chicken from the saucepan with kitchen tongs to a cutting board. Using 2 forks, shred the chicken. Return the chicken to the saucepan and heat through. Divide the chicken mixture among the buns. Sprinkle with the cheese.

Cranberry Apple Bread Pudding

MAKES: 6 SERVINGS

PREP: 10 MINUTES

STAND: 20 MINUTES

BAKE: 40 MINUTES

Vegetable cooking spray

4 cups Pepperidge Farm® Cubed Unseasoned **or** Herb Seasoned Stuffing

¾ cup dried cranberries

4 eggs

2½ cups milk

½ cup granulated sugar

½ cup chunky sweetened applesauce

1 teaspoon vanilla extract

Brandied Butter Sauce

MAKE AHEAD

The Bread Pudding and Brandied Butter Sauce can both be assembled 1 day ahead. Cover and refrigerate. Remove the pudding from refrigerator to come to room temperature while the oven preheats. To reheat the sauce, microwave in a microwavable cup on MEDIUM for 1 minute or until it's hot.

1. Heat the oven to 350°F. Spray an 11×8-inch (2-quart) baking dish with cooking spray. Place the stuffing in the prepared dish. Sprinkle the cranberries over the stuffing.

2. Beat the eggs, milk, sugar, applesauce and vanilla with a fork or whisk in a medium bowl. Pour over the stuffing mixture. Let stand for 20 minutes.

3. Bake at 350°F. for 40 minutes or until knife inserted near the center comes out clean. Serve warm with *Brandied Butter Sauce*.

Brandied Butter Sauce: Heat ½ **cup (1 stick) butter** in a 1-quart saucepan over medium heat until the butter melts. Add ½ **cup** packed light brown sugar. Cook and stir until the sugar dissolves and the mixture is bubbly. Remove from the heat. Whisk in **2 tablespoons** brandy. Makes 1 cup.

Creamy Corn Pudding

MAKES: 6 SERVINGS

Butter

1 can (10¾ ounces) Campbell's® Condensed Cream of Chicken Soup (Regular **or** 98% Fat Free)

½ cup milk

2 eggs

1 can (16 ounces) whole kernel corn, drained

½ cup cornmeal

¼ cup grated Parmesan cheese

1 tablespoon chopped fresh chives

PREP: 10 MINUTES

BAKE: 35 MINUTES

1. Heat the oven to 350°F. Butter a 1½-quart casserole.

2. Beat the soup, milk and eggs with a whisk or fork in a medium bowl. Stir in the corn, cornmeal, cheese and chives. Pour the soup mixture into the prepared casserole.

3. Bake for 35 minutes or until puffed and golden brown.

Sausage and Broccoli Skillet

MAKES: 6 SERVINGS

PREP: 5 MINUTES

COOK: 25 MINUTES

1½ pounds sweet Italian pork sausage, casing removed

1 medium onion, chopped (about ½ cup)

2 cloves garlic, minced

1 can (10¾ ounces) Campbell's® Condensed Cream of Broccoli Soup (Regular **or** 98% Fat Free)

½ cup milk

1 bag (about 16 ounces) frozen broccoli cuts

½ cup shredded Parmesan cheese

4½ cups corkscrew-shaped pasta, cooked and drained

Crushed red pepper (optional)

1. Cook the sausage in a 6-quart saucepot over medium-high heat until the sausage is well browned, stirring frequently to break up meat.

2. Reduce the heat to medium. Add the onion and garlic to the saucepot and cook until tender. Pour off any fat.

3. Stir the soup, milk, broccoli and **¼ cup** of the cheese into the saucepot. Heat to a boil. Reduce the heat to low. Cover and cook for 5 minutes or until the broccoli is tender, stirring occasionally.

4. Put the pasta in a large serving bowl. Pour the sausage mixture over the pasta. Toss to coat. Sprinkle with the remaining cheese. Serve with red pepper, if desired.

3-Step Family Favorites

Favorite dishes prepared in just 3 steps

Savory Chicken Thighs with Figs

MAKES: 6 SERVINGS

PREP: 5 MINUTES

COOK: 30 MINUTES

1½ pounds skinless, boneless chicken thighs

2 tablespoons all-purpose flour

1 tablespoon olive oil

1 medium onion, chopped (about ½ cup)

2 cloves garlic, minced

1 cup Swanson® Chicken Broth (Regular, Natural Goodness™ **or** Certified Organic)

2 tablespoons balsamic vinegar

1 teaspoon dried thyme leaves, crushed

6 ounces dried figs, stems removed and cut in half

Hot cooked rice

1. Coat the chicken with the flour.

2. Heat the oil in a 10-inch skillet over medium-high heat. Add the chicken in 2 batches and cook until it's well browned on both sides.

3. Add the onion and garlic and cook until tender. Stir the broth, vinegar, thyme and figs into the skillet. Heat to a boil. Reduce the heat to low. Cover and cook for 10 minutes or until the chicken is cooked through. Serve with rice.

Sun-Dried Tomato Bow Tie Pasta

MAKES: 4 SERVINGS

PREP: 5 MINUTES

COOK: 20 MINUTES

1   tablespoon olive oil

1   large sweet onion, finely chopped (about 1 cup)

⅓ cup oil-packed sun-dried tomatoes, cut into thin strips

2   cloves garlic, minced

1   can (10¾ ounces) Campbell's® Condensed Cream of Chicken Soup (Regular **or** 98% Fat Free)

1   cup milk

2   tablespoons thinly sliced basil leaves

1   package (16 ounces) bow tie-shaped pasta (farfalle), cooked and drained

2   tablespoons grated Parmesan cheese

Freshly ground black pepper (optional)

CAMPBELL'S KITCHEN

For a thinner sauce, reserve ¼ cup of the pasta cooking water and add it to the skillet with the soup and milk.

1. Heat the oil in a 10-inch skillet over medium heat. Add the onion and cook until tender.

2. Add the tomatoes and garlic and cook for 1 minute. Stir the soup, milk and basil into the skillet. Cook until the mixture is hot and bubbling, stirring occasionally.

3. Put the pasta in a large serving bowl. Pour the soup mixture over the pasta and toss to coat. Sprinkle with the cheese. Sprinkle with black pepper, if desired.

Buffalo Burgers

MAKES: 4 SERVINGS

PREP: 10 MINUTES

COOK: 20 MINUTES

CAMPBELL'S KITCHEN

Any leftover soup mixture can also be a great dipping sauce for French fries.

1 pound ground beef

1 can (10¾ ounces) Campbell's® Condensed Tomato Soup

½ teaspoon Louisiana-style hot sauce

4 hamburger rolls, split

Lettuce leaves, red onion slices, tomato slices (optional)

½ cup crumbled blue cheese

1. Shape the beef into 4 (½-inch-thick) burgers.

2. Heat the soup and hot sauce in a 1-quart saucepan over medium heat. Heat to a boil. Reduce the heat to low. Cover and cook for 5 minutes. Keep warm.

3. Lightly oil the grill rack and heat the grill to medium. Grill the burgers for 10 minutes for medium or until desired doneness, turning over halfway through cooking. Serve the burgers on rolls with lettuce, onion and tomato, if desired. Top with the soup mixture. Sprinkle with the cheese.

Asian Chicken & Rice Bake

MAKES: 4 SERVINGS

PREP: 5 MINUTES

BAKE: 45 MINUTES

CAMPBELL'S KITCHEN

Add 2 cups frozen broccoli to the rice before baking. Serve with your favorite stir-fry vegetable blend.

¾ cup **uncooked** regular long-grain white rice

4 skinless, boneless chicken breast halves

1 can (10¾ ounces) Campbell's® Condensed Golden Mushroom Soup

¾ cup water

2 tablespoons soy sauce

2 tablespoons cider vinegar

2 tablespoons honey

1 teaspoon garlic powder

Paprika

1. Spread the rice in an 11×8-inch (2-quart) shallow baking dish. Top with the chicken.

2. Stir the soup, water, soy sauce, vinegar, honey and garlic powder in a medium bowl. Pour the soup mixture over the chicken. Sprinkle with the paprika. **Cover**.

3. Bake at 375°F. for 45 minutes or until the chicken is cooked through.

Southern Turkey Cornbread Pot Pie

PREP: 5 MINUTES

COOK: 5 MINUTES

BAKE: 15 MINUTES

EASY SUBSTITUTION

Substitute cooked chicken for the turkey.

1   can (10¾ ounces) Campbell's® Condensed Cream of Chicken Soup (Regular **or** 98% Fat Free)

⅛   teaspoon ground black pepper

2   cups cubed cooked turkey

1   can (about 8 ounces) whole kernel corn, drained

1   package (11 ounces) refrigerated cornbread twists

1. Heat the oven to 425°F.

2. Heat the soup, black pepper, turkey and corn in a 2-quart saucepan over medium heat until the mixture is hot and bubbling. Pour the turkey mixture into a 9-inch pie plate.

3. Separate the cornbread into **8** pieces along perforations. (Do not unroll dough.) Place over the hot turkey mixture. Bake for 15 minutes or until the bread is golden.

Honey Mustard Chicken

MAKES: 4 SERVINGS

PREP: 5 MINUTES

COOK: 20 MINUTES

2 tablespoons cornstarch

1¾ cups Swanson® Chicken Broth (Regular, Natural Goodness™ **or** Certified Organic)

1 tablespoon honey

1 tablespoon Dijon mustard

Vegetable cooking spray

4 skinless, boneless chicken breast halves

1 large carrot, cut into 2-inch matchstick-thin strips (about 1 cup)

1 medium onion, sliced (about ½ cup)

Hot cooked rice (optional)

CAMPBELL'S
KITCHEN

For a more flavorful rice side dish, cook the rice in Swanson® Chicken Broth instead of water according to the package directions, and then there is no need to add salt or butter.

1. Stir the cornstarch, broth, honey and mustard in a small bowl. Set the mixture aside.

2. Spray a 10-inch skillet with cooking spray. Heat over medium-high heat for 1 minute. Add the chicken and cook for 10 minutes or until it's browned on both sides.

3. Add the carrot and onion. Reduce the heat to low. Cover and cook for 5 minutes or until the chicken is cooked through and the vegetables are tender-crisp. Stir the cornstarch mixture and stir it into the skillet. Cook and stir until the mixture boils and thickens. Serve with the rice, if desired.

Rosemary Chicken & Mushroom Pasta

MAKES: 6 SERVINGS

PREP: 10 MINUTES

COOK: 20 MINUTES

2   tablespoons olive **or** vegetable oil

1½ pounds skinless, boneless chicken breasts, cut into strips

4   cups sliced mushrooms (about 12 ounces)

1   tablespoon minced garlic

1   tablespoon chopped fresh rosemary leaves **or** 1 teaspoon dried rosemary leaves, crushed

1   can (14½ ounces) Campbell's® Chicken Gravy

1   package (16 ounces) linguine **or** spaghetti, cooked and drained

   Shredded Parmesan cheese

1. Heat the oil in a 12-inch skillet over medium-high heat. Add the chicken and mushrooms and cook in 2 batches or until it's well browned, stirring often. Remove the chicken and mushrooms and set them aside.

2. Reduce the heat to low. Stir the garlic and rosemary into the skillet and cook for 1 minute. Stir the gravy into the skillet. Heat to a boil.

3. Return the chicken and mushrooms to the skillet. Cover and cook for 5 minutes or until the chicken is cooked through. Place the pasta in a large serving bowl. Pour the chicken mixture over the pasta. Toss to coat. Serve with the cheese.

Pan-Seared Beef Steaks with Garlic Red Wine Gravy

MAKES: 8 SERVINGS

PREP: 10 MINUTES

COOK: 15 MINUTES

EASY SUBSTITUTION

Another red wine to use instead of the Burgundy would be a Cabernet Sauvignon, Merlot or Pinot Noir.

3 teaspoons butter

8 filet mignons (tenderloin steaks), ¾-inch thick (about 5 ounces **each**)

½ cup chopped shallots **or** onion

1 clove garlic, minced

1 can (10¼ ounces) Campbell's® Beef Gravy

½ cup Burgundy **or** other dry red wine

Sliced fresh chives (optional)

1. Heat **1 teaspoon** of the butter in a 12-inch skillet over high heat. Add **4** steaks and cook for 2 minutes on each side for medium-rare or to desired doneness. Remove the steaks from the skillet to a serving platter. Cover and keep warm. Repeat with **1 teaspoon** of the butter and the remaining steaks.

2. Reduce the heat to medium. Add the remaining butter. Add the shallots and cook for 1 minute. Add the garlic and cook for 30 seconds.

3. Stir the gravy and wine into the skillet. Heat to a boil. Return the steaks to the skillet and heat through. Serve with sliced chives, if desired.

Cornbread Chicken Pot Pie

MAKES: 4 SERVINGS

PREP: 10 MINUTES

BAKE: 30 MINUTES

1 can (10¾ ounces) Campbell's® Condensed Cream of Chicken Soup (Regular **or** 98% Fat Free)

1 can (about 8 ounces) whole kernel corn, drained

2 cups cubed cooked chicken **or** turkey

1 package (8½ ounces) corn muffin mix

¾ cup milk

1 egg

½ cup shredded Cheddar cheese

1. Heat the oven to 400°F. Stir the soup, corn and chicken in a 9-inch pie plate.

2. Stir the muffin mix, milk and egg with a fork in a small bowl until the ingredients are mixed. Spoon over the chicken mixture.

3. Bake for 30 minutes or until the cornbread is golden. Sprinkle with the cheese.

Whole Grain Huevos Rancheros

MAKES: 4 SERVINGS

¾ cup Pace® Chunky Salsa

Vegetable cooking spray

4 eggs

4 Pepperidge Farm® Whole Grain English Muffins,
  split and toasted

½ cup shredded Mexican cheese blend

4 teaspoons chopped fresh cilantro **or** parsley

PREP: 5 MINUTES

COOK: 15 MINUTES

1. Heat the salsa in a 1-quart saucepan over medium heat until it's hot, stirring occasionally. Cover and keep warm.

2. Spray a 10-inch skillet with cooking spray and heat over medium heat for 1 minute. Crack the eggs and add to the skillet one at a time. Cook until the whites are firm or to desired doneness.

3. Divide the muffin halves among **4** serving plates. Top each open-faced muffin with **1** egg, **3 tablespoons** of the salsa, **2 tablespoons** of the cheese and **about 1 teaspoon** of the cilantro.

Scalloped Apple Bake

MAKES: 6 SERVINGS

PREP: 25 MINUTES

BAKE: 40 MINUTES

4 tablespoons butter, melted

¼ cup sugar

2 teaspoons grated orange peel

1 teaspoon ground cinnamon

1½ cups Pepperidge Farm® Corn Bread Stuffing

½ cup pecan halves, coarsely chopped

1 can (16 ounces) whole berry cranberry sauce

⅓ cup orange juice **or** water

4 large cooking apples, cored and thinly sliced (about 6 cups)

1. Mix the butter, sugar, orange peel, cinnamon, stuffing and pecans in a 1-quart bowl. Set the mixture aside.

2. Mix the cranberry sauce, juice and apples in a 3-quart bowl. Add **half** of the stuffing mixture and stir lightly to coat. Spoon into an 8-inch square baking dish. Sprinkle the remaining stuffing mixture over the apple mixture.

3. Bake at 375°F. for 40 minutes or until the apples are tender.

Sloppy Joes Italiano

MAKES: 6 SANDWICHES

1	pound ground beef
2	cups Prego® Italian Sauce, any variety
¼	cup grated Parmesan cheese
6	hamburger rolls, split

PREP: 5 MINUTES

COOK: 15 MINUTES

1. Cook the beef in a 10-inch skillet over medium-high heat until the beef is well browned, stirring frequently to break up the meat. Pour off any fat.

2. Stir the sauce and cheese into the skillet. Cook until the mixture is hot and bubbling.

3. Divide the beef mixture among the rolls.

Super Chunky Fudge

PREP: 15 MINUTES

COOK: 10 MINUTES

CHILL: 2 HOURS

1 bag (5.1 ounces) Pepperidge Farm® Mini Chocolate Chunk Cookies, coarsely crumbled (about 2 cups)

1 cup miniature marshmallows

Vegetable cooking spray

3 cups semi-sweet chocolate pieces (18 ounces)

1 can (14 ounces) sweetened condensed milk

⅛ teaspoon salt

1 teaspoon vanilla extract

1. Reserve ½ **cup** of the crumbled cookies and ¼ **cup** of the marshmallows. Line an 8-inch square baking pan with foil. Spray the foil with cooking spray. Heat the chocolate, milk and salt in a 2-quart saucepan over low heat until the chocolate melts, stirring often.

2. Remove the chocolate mixture from the heat and stir in the remaining crumbled cookies, remaining marshmallows and vanilla. Spread the mixture evenly into the prepared pan. Press the reserved cookies and marshmallows into top of the fudge.

3. Refrigerate for 2 hours or until firm. Remove the fudge from the pan and peel away foil. Cut into 16 squares. Cover with foil. Store in the refrigerator.

Raspberry Tiramisù

MAKES: 6 SERVINGS

PREP: 20 MINUTES

CHILL: 1 HOUR

1   package (8 ounces) cream cheese, softened
1   cup confectioners' sugar
¼   teaspoon ground cinnamon
1   cup heavy cream, whipped
1   package (6 ounces) Pepperidge Farm® Milano® Distinctive Cookies
⅓   cup brewed black coffee
1   cup sweetened frozen raspberries, thawed and drained
¼   cup grated semi-sweet chocolate for garnish

1. Beat the cream cheese in a medium bowl with an electric mixer on medium speed until smooth. Beat in the sugar and cinnamon. Stir in the whipped cream.

2. Spoon **1 cup** cheese mixture into a 4-cup trifle bowl. Dip **6** of the cookies, one at a time, into the coffee and place over the cheese layer, overlapping slightly. Spoon **2 tablespoons** of the raspberries over the cookies. Repeat the layers once. Spread the remaining cheese mixture over the top. Garnish with the remaining cookies and raspberries. Refrigerate for at least 1 hour.

3. Garnish with the chocolate before serving.

Brothy Shrimp & Rice Scampi

MAKES: 4 SERVINGS

PREP: 15 MINUTES

COOK: 25 MINUTES

3½ cups Swanson® Chicken Broth (Regular, Natural Goodness™ **or** Certified Organic)

¾ cup **uncooked** regular long-grain white rice

1 tablespoon olive oil

1 pound fresh **or** frozen large shrimp, shelled and deveined

4 cloves garlic, minced

2 tablespoons lemon juice

2 medium green onions, thinly sliced (about ¼ cup)

1. Heat the broth in a 2-quart saucepan over high heat to a boil. Stir in the rice. Reduce the heat to low. Cover and cook for 20 minutes.

2. Heat the oil in a 10-inch skillet over medium-high heat. Add the shrimp and garlic. Cook and stir for 5 minutes or until the shrimp turn pink.

3. Divide the shrimp among **4** serving bowls. Stir the lemon juice into the rice mixture and pour over the shrimp. Top with the green onions.

Savory Meatloaf

1½   pounds ground beef

1   can (10¾ ounces) Campbell's® Condensed Tomato Soup

½   cup dry bread crumbs

1   egg, beaten

1   small onion, finely chopped (about ¼ cup)

1   tablespoon Worcestershire sauce

⅛   teaspoon ground black pepper

¼   cup water

PREP: 15 MINUTES

BAKE: 1 HOUR

COOK: 5 MINUTES

1. Thoroughly mix the beef, **½ cup** of the soup, bread crumbs, egg, onion, Worcestershire sauce and black pepper. Put the mixture into a 13×9-inch baking pan and firmly shape into an 8×4-inch loaf.

2. Bake at 350°F. for 1 hour or until the meatloaf is cooked through. Remove the meatloaf from the pan to a cutting board.

3. Heat **2 tablespoons** of the pan drippings, the remaining soup and water in a 1-quart saucepan over medium-high heat until the mixture is hot and bubbling. Serve with the meatloaf.

Index

METRIC CONVERSION CHART

VOLUME MEASUREMENTS (dry)

1/8 teaspoon = 0.5 mL
1/4 teaspoon = 1 mL
1/2 teaspoon = 2 mL
3/4 teaspoon = 4 mL
1 teaspoon = 5 mL
1 tablespoon = 15 mL
2 tablespoons = 30 mL
1/4 cup = 60 mL
1/3 cup = 75 mL
1/2 cup = 125 mL
2/3 cup = 150 mL
3/4 cup = 175 mL
1 cup = 250 mL
2 cups = 1 pint = 500 mL
3 cups = 750 mL
4 cups = 1 quart = 1 L

VOLUME MEASUREMENTS (fluid)

1 fluid ounce (2 tablespoons) = 30 mL
4 fluid ounces (1/2 cup) = 125 mL
8 fluid ounces (1 cup) = 250 mL
12 fluid ounces (1 1/2 cups) = 375 mL
16 fluid ounces (2 cups) = 500 mL

WEIGHTS (mass)

1/2 ounce = 15 g
1 ounce = 30 g
3 ounces = 90 g
4 ounces = 120 g
8 ounces = 225 g
10 ounces = 285 g
12 ounces = 360 g
16 ounces = 1 pound = 450 g

DIMENSIONS

1/16 inch = 2 mm
1/8 inch = 3 mm
1/4 inch = 6 mm
1/2 inch = 1.5 cm
3/4 inch = 2 cm
1 inch = 2.5 cm

OVEN TEMPERATURES

250°F = 120°C
275°F = 140°C
300°F = 150°C
325°F = 160°C
350°F = 180°C
375°F = 190°C
400°F = 200°C
425°F = 220°C
450°F = 230°C

BAKING PAN AND DISH EQUIVALENTS

Utensil	Size in Inches	Size in Centimeters	Volume	Metric Volume
Baking or Cake Pan (square or rectangular)	8×8×2	20×20×5	8 cups	2 L
	9×9×2	23×23×5	10 cups	2.5 L
	13×9×2	33×23×5	12 cups	3 L
Loaf Pan	8 1/2×4 1/2×2 1/2	21×11×6	6 cups	1.5 L
	9×9×3	23×13×7	8 cups	2 L
Round Layer Cake Pan	8×1 1/2	20×4	4 cups	1 L
	9×1 1/2	23×4	5 cups	1.25
Pie Plate	8×1 1/2	20×4	4 cups	1 L
	9×1 1/2	23×4	5 cups	1.25
Baking Dish or Casserole			1 quart/4 cups	1 L
			1 1/2 quart/6 cups	1.5 L
			2 quart/8 cups	2 L
			3 quart/12 cups	3 L